THE LITTLE LIBRARY OF EARTH MEDICINE

DEER

Kenneth Meadows

Illustrations by Jo Donegan

DK PUBLISHING, INC.

A DK PUBLISHING BOOK

The Little Library of Earth Medicine was
produced, edited, and designed by
GLS Editorial and Design
Garden Studios, 11-15 Betterton Street
London WC2H 9BP

Editorial director: Jane Laing
Design director: Ruth Shane
Project designer: Luke Herriott
Editors: Claire Calman, Terry Burrows, Victoria Sorzano
US Editors: Jennifer Dorr, William Lach, Barbara Minton

Additional illustrations: Roy Flooks 16, 17, 31; John Lawrence 38
Special photography: Mark Hamilton
Picture credits: American Natural History Museum 8-9, 12, 14-15, 32

First American Edition, 1998
2 4 6 8 10 9 7 5 3 1

Published in the United States by DK Publishing, Inc.
95 Madison Avenue, New York, NY 10016
Visit us on the World Wide Web at http://www.dk.com

Library of Congress Cataloging-in-Publication Data
Meadows, Kenneth.
    The little library of earth medicine / by Kenneth Meadows. – 1st American ed.
        p.   cm.
    Contents: |1| Falcon, 21st March-19th April – |2| Beaver, 20th April-20 May – |3|
Deer, 21st May-20th June – |4| Woodpecker, 21st June-21st July – |5| Salmon, 22nd July-
21st August – |6| Brown Bear, 22nd August-21st September – |7| Crow, 22nd
September-22nd October – |8| Snake, 23rd October-22nd November – |9| Owl, 23rd
November-21st December – |10| Goose, 22nd December-19 January – |11| Otter, 20th
January-18th February – |12| Wolf, 19th February-20th March.
    Includes indexes.
    ISBN 0-7894-2886-5
    1. Medicine wheels–Miscellanea. 2. Horoscopes. 3. Indians of North
America–Religion–Miscellanea. 4. Typology (Psychology)–Miscellanea. I. Title.
BF1623.M43M42 1998
133.5'9397–dc21   97-42267
                                                                                                          CIP

Reproduced by Kestrel Digital Colour Ltd, Chelmsford, Essex
Printed and bound in Hong Kong by Imago

CONTENTS

INTRODUCING
EARTH MEDICINE

To Native Americans, medicine is not an external
substance but an inner power that is found in
both Nature and ourselves.

Earth Medicine is a unique
method of personality
profiling that draws on
Native American under-
standing of the Universe, and
on the principles embodied in
sacred Medicine Wheels.

Native Americans believed
that spirit, although invisible,
permeated Nature, so that
everything in Nature was
sacred. Animals were
perceived as acting as

messengers of spirit. They
also appeared in waking
dreams to impart power
known as "medicine." The
recipients of such dreams
honored the animal species
that appeared to them by
rendering their images on
ceremonial, ornamental,
and everyday artifacts.

NATURE WITHIN SELF

Native American shamans
– tribal wisemen –
recognized similarities
between the natural forces
prevalent during the seasons and
the characteristics of those born

Shaman's rattle
*Shamans used rattles to connect
with their inner spirit. This is a
Tlingit shaman's wooden rattle.*

*"Spirit has provided you with an opportunity to
study in Nature's university."* Stoney teaching

8

during corresponding times of the year. They also noted how personality is affected by the four phases of the Moon – at birth and throughout life – and by the continual alternation of energy flow, from active to passive. This view is encapsulated in Earth Medicine, which helps you to recognize how the dynamics of Nature function within you and how the potential strengths you were born with can be developed.

Animal ornament
To the Anasazi, who carved this ornament from jet, the frog symbolized adaptability.

MEDICINE WHEELS

Native American cultural traditions embrace a variety of circular symbolic images and objects. These sacred hoops have become known as Medicine

Feast dish
Stylized bear carvings adorn this Tlingit feast dish. To the Native American, the bear symbolizes strength and self-sufficiency.

Wheels, due to their similarity to the spoked wheels of the wagons that carried settlers into the heartlands of once-Native American territory. Each Medicine Wheel showed how different objects or qualities related to one another within the context of a greater whole, and how different forces and energies moved within it.

One Medicine Wheel might be regarded as the master wheel because it indicated balance within Nature and the most effective way of achieving harmony with the Universe and ourselves. It is upon this master Medicine Wheel (see pp.10–11) that Earth Medicine is structured.

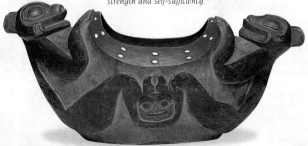

THE MEDICINE WHEEL

The outer Wheel is divided into twelve birth times, each of which has its own animal totem, and stone, tree, and colour affinities.

At the hub of the Wheel, surrounded by representations of Elements, Directions, and energy flow, is the Wakan-Tanka – symbol of invisible energies coming into physical reality.

Season of birth
Each of the twelve segments relates to a specific time of year (see pp.12–13).

Wakan-Tanka
The powerful symbol used by some Native Americans to denote energy coming into form (see p.24).

NORTH: WINTER

WEST: AUTUMN

WOLF

OTTER

GOOSE

OWL

SNAKE

CROW

Stone affinity
Each birth time has a particular stone associated with it (see pp.14–15).

Tree affinity
Each birth time is connected to a type of tree (see pp.14–15).

Birth totem
An animal totem represents each birth time (see pp.16–17).

Directional totem
One of four cardinal Directions exerts an influence on each birth time (see pp.18–19).

Principal Element
Each birth time is fundamentally influenced by one of the four Elements (see pp.20–21).

Elemental Aspect
Each birth time has its own Elemental Aspect (see pp.20–21).

Energy flow
Energy alternates between active and receptive with each birth time (see p.24).

EAST: SPRING

SOUTH: SUMMER

FALCON

BEAVER

DEER

DEER

WOODPECKER

SALMON

BROWN BEAR

THE TWELVE
BIRTH TIMES

THE STRUCTURE OF THE MEDICINE WHEEL IS BASED UPON THE SEASONS TO REFLECT THE POWERFUL INFLUENCE OF NATURE ON HUMAN PERSONALITY.

he Medicine Wheel classifies human nature into twelve personality types, each corresponding to the characteristics of Nature at a particular time of the year. It is designed to act as a kind of map to help you discover your strengths and weaknesses, your inner drives and instinctive behaviors, and your true potential.

The four seasons form the basis of the Wheel's structure, with the Summer and Winter solstices and the Spring and Autumn equinoxes marking each season's passing. In Earth Medicine,

each season is a metaphor for a stage of human growth and development. Spring is likened to infancy and the newness of life, and Summer to the exuberance of youth and of rapid development. Autumn represents the fulfillment that mature adulthood brings, while Winter symbolizes the accumulated wisdom that can be drawn upon in later life.

Each seasonal quarter of the Wheel is further divided into three periods, making twelve time segments altogether. The time of your birth determines the direction from which

Seasonal rites

Performers at the Iroquois mid-Winter ceremony wore masks made of braided maize husks. They danced to attune themselves to energies that would ensure a good harvest.

SPRING EQUINOX

AWAKENING

BLUSTERY WINDS

NORTH

CLEANSING

EAST

GROWING

RENEWAL

FLOWERING

SUMMER SOLSTICE

LONG DAYS

LONG NIGHTS

WEST

FROST

FALLING LEAVES

HARVESTING

RIPENING

SOUTH

AUTUMN EQUINOX

THE TWELVE TIME SEGMENTS

you perceive life, and the qualities imbued in Nature in that season are reflected in your core character.

Each of the twelve time segments, or birth times, is named after a feature in the natural yearly cycle. For example, the period after the Spring equinox is called Awakening time because it is the time of new growth, while the segment after the Autumn equinox is named after the falling leaves that characterize that time.

THE SIGNIFICANCE OF
TOTEMS

NATIVE AMERICANS BELIEVED THAT TOTEMS — ANIMAL
SYMBOLS — REPRESENTED ESSENTIAL TRUTHS AND ACTED
AS CONNECTIONS TO NATURAL POWERS.

A totem is an animal or natural object adopted as an emblem to typify certain distinctive qualities. Native Americans regarded animals, whose behavior is predictable, as particularly useful guides to categorizing human patterns of behavior.

A totem mirrors aspects of your nature and unlocks the intuitive knowledge that lies beyond the reasoning capacity of the intellect. It may take the form of a carving or molding, a pictorial image, or a token of fur, feather, bone, tooth, or claw. Its presence serves as an immediate link with the energies it represents. A totem is therefore more effective than a glyph or symbol as an aid to comprehending nonphysical powers and formative forces.

PRIMARY TOTEMS

In Earth Medicine you have three primary totems: a birth totem, a Directional totem, and an Elemental totem. Your *birth totem* is the embodiment of core characteristics that correspond with the dominant aspects of Nature during your birth time.

Symbol of strength

The handle of this Tlingit knife is carved with a raven and a bear head, symbols of insight and inner strength.

All twelve birth totems, each relating to a birth time, are described on pp.16–17.

Your *Directional totem* aligns you with your inner senses, which direct the main thrust of your endeavors. Each of the four seasons on the Wheel is compatible with one of the four Directions, and each of the Directions is represented by a totem. For example, Spring is associated with the East, where the sun rises, and signifies seeing things in new ways; its totem is the Eagle. The four

Prize totem

A chief or warrior of the Fox tribe affirmed his rank with this bear claw necklace.

Directional totems are explained on pp.18–19.

Your *Elemental totem* relates to your instinctive behaviors. The qualities of the four Elements – Fire, Water, Earth, and Air – and their totems are introduced on pp.20–21.

THREE AFFINITIES

Each birth time also has an affinity with a tree, a stone, and a color (see pp.36–41). These three affinities have qualities that can strengthen you during challenging times.

> "If a man is to succeed, he must be governed not by his inclination, but by an understanding of the ways of animals..." *Teton Sioux teaching*

THE TWELVE
BIRTH TOTEMS

THE TWELVE BIRTH TIMES ARE REPRESENTED BY TOTEMS,
EACH ONE AN ANIMAL THAT BEST EXPRESSES THE
QUALITIES INHERENT IN THAT BIRTH TIME.

Earth Medicine associates an animal totem with each birth time (the two sets of dates below reflect the difference in season between the Northern and Southern Hemispheres). These animals help to connect you to the powers and abilities that they represent. For an in-depth study of the Deer birth totem, see pp.28–29.

FALCON
March 21 – April 19 (N. Hem)
Sept 22 – Oct 22 (S. Hem)
Falcons are full of initiative, but often rush in to make decisions they may later regret. Lively and extroverted, they have enthusiasm for new experiences but can sometimes lack persistence.

DEER
May 21 – June 20 (N. Hem)
Nov 23 – Dec 21 (S. Hem)
Deer are willing to sacrifice the old for the new. They loathe routine, thriving on variety and challenges. They have a wild side, often leaping from one situation or relationship into another without reflection.

BEAVER
April 20 – May 20 (N. Hem)
Oct 23 – Nov 22 (S. Hem)
Practical and steady, Beavers have a capacity for perseverance. Good homemakers, they are warm and affectionate but need harmony and peace to avoid becoming irritable. They have a keen aesthetic sense.

WOODPECKER
June 21 – July 21 (N. Hem)
Dec 22 – Jan 19 (S. Hem)
Emotional and sensitive, Woodpeckers are warm to those closest to them, and willing to sacrifice their needs for those of their loved ones. They have lively imaginations but can be worriers.

SALMON

July 22 – August 21 (N. Hem)
Jan 20 – Feb 18 (S. Hem)

Enthusiastic and self-confident, Salmon people enjoy running things. They are uncompromising and forceful, and can occasionally seem a little arrogant or self-important. They are easily hurt by neglect.

OWL

Nov 23 – Dec 21 (N. Hem)
May 21 – June 20 (S. Hem)

Owls need freedom of expression. They are lively, self-reliant, and have an eye for detail. Inquisitive and adaptable, they have a tendency to overextend themselves. Owls are often physically courageous.

BROWN BEAR

August 22 – Sept 21 (N. Hem)
Feb 19 – March 20 (S. Hem)

Brown Bears are hardworking, practical, and self-reliant. They do not like change, preferring to stick to what is familiar. They have a flair for fixing things, are good-natured, and make good friends.

GOOSE

Dec 22 – Jan 19 (N. Hem)
June 21 – July 21 (S. Hem)

Goose people are far-sighted idealists who are willing to explore the unknown. They approach life with enthusiasm, determined to fulfill their dreams. They are perfectionists, and can appear unduly serious.

CROW

Sept 22 – Oct 22 (N. Hem)
March 21 – April 19 (S. Hem)

Crows dislike solitude and feel most comfortable in company. Although usually pleasant and good-natured, they can be strongly influenced by negative atmospheres, becoming gloomy and prickly.

OTTER

Jan 20 – Feb 18 (N. Hem)
July 22 – August 21 (S. Hem)

Otters are friendly, lively, and perceptive. They feel inhibited by too many rules and regulations, which often makes them appear eccentric. They like cleanliness and order, and have original minds.

SNAKE

Oct 23 – Nov 22 (N. Hem)
April 20 – May 20 (S. Hem)

Snakes are secretive and mysterious, hiding their feelings beneath a cool exterior. Adaptable, determined, and imaginative, they are capable of bouncing back from tough situations encountered in life.

WOLF

Feb 19 – March 20 (N. Hem)
August 22 – Sept 21 (S. Hem)

Wolves are sensitive, artistic, and intuitive – people to whom others turn for help. They value freedom and their own space, and are easily affected by others. They are philosophical, trusting, and genuine.

THE INFLUENCE OF THE
DIRECTIONS

ALSO KNOWN BY NATIVE AMERICANS AS THE FOUR
WINDS, THE INFLUENCE OF THE FOUR DIRECTIONS IS
EXPERIENCED THROUGH YOUR INNER SENSES.

Regarded as the "keepers" or "caretakers" of the Universe, the four Directions or alignments were also referred to by Native Americans as the four Winds because their presence was felt rather than seen.

DIRECTIONAL TOTEMS

In Earth Medicine, each Direction or Wind is associated with a season and a time of day. Thus the three Spring birth times – Awakening time, Growing time, and Flowering time –

all fall within the East Direction, and morning. The Direction to which you birth time belongs influences the nature of your inner senses.

The East Direction is associated with illumination. Its totem is the Eagle – a bird that soars closest to the Sun and can see clearly from height. The South is the Direction of Summer and the afternoon. It signifies growth and fruition, fluidity, and emotions. Its totem, the Mouse, symbolizes productivity, feelings, and an ability to perceive detail.

"Remember...the circle of the sky, the stars, the super-natural Winds breathing night and day...the four Directions." Pawnee teaching

SPRING EQUINOX

NORTH

EAST

SUMMER SOLSTICE

BUFFALO

EAGLE

The four Directions

Each Direction is associated with a season and a time of day, and also with a principal function: the East with determining, the South with giving, the West with holding, and the North with receiving.

GRIZZLY BEAR

MOUSE

WEST

SOUTH

AUTUMN EQUINOX

The West is the Direction of Autumn and the evening. It signifies transformation – from day to night, from Summer to Winter – and the qualities of introspection and conservation. Its totem is the Grizzly Bear, which represents strength drawn from within. The North is the Direction of Winter and the night, and is associated with the mind and its sustenance – knowledge. Its totem is the Buffalo, an animal that was honored by Native Americans as the great material "provider."

THE INFLUENCE OF THE ELEMENTS

THE FOUR ELEMENTS – AIR, FIRE, WATER, AND EARTH –
PERVADE EVERYTHING AND INDICATE THE NATURE OF
MOVEMENT AND THE ESSENCE OF WHO YOU ARE.

lements are intangible qualities
that describe the essential state
or character of all things. In
Earth Medicine, the four Elements are
allied with four fundamental modes
of activity and are associated with
different aspects of the self. Air
expresses free movement in all
directions; it is related to the
mind and to thinking. Fire
indicates expansive
motion; it is linked with
the spirit and with
intuition. Water
signifies fluidity; it

Elemental profile
*The Elemental config-
uration of Deer is Air of
Fire. Fire is the Principal
Element and Air the
Elemental Aspect.*

WATER

AIR

EARTH

FIRE

has associations with the soul and the emotions. Earth symbolizes stability; it is related to the physical body and the sensations.

ELEMENTAL DISTRIBUTION

On the Medicine Wheel one Element is associated with each of the four Directions – Fire in the East, Earth in the West, Air in the North, and Water in the South. These are known as the Principal Elements.

The four Elements also have an individual association with each of the twelve birth times – known as the Elemental Aspects. They follow a cyclical sequence around the Wheel based on the action of the Sun (Fire) on the Earth, producing atmosphere (Air) and condensation (Water).

The three birth times that share an Elemental Aspect belong to the same Elemental family or "clan," with a totem that gives insight into its key characteristics. Deer people belong to the Butterfly clan (see pp.34–35).

ELEMENTAL EMPHASIS

For each birth time, the qualities of the Elemental Aspect usually predominate over those of the Principal Element, although both are present to give a specific configuration, such as Fire of Earth (for Deer's, see pp.34–35). For Falcon, Woodpecker, and Otter, the Principal Element and the Elemental Aspect are identical (for example, Air of Air), so people of these totems tend to express that Element intensely.

FIRE

EARTH

AIR

WATER

THE INFLUENCE OF THE MOON

THE WAXING AND WANING OF THE MOON DURING ITS
FOUR PHASES HAS A CRUCIAL INFLUENCE ON THE
FORMATION OF PERSONALITY AND HUMAN ENDEAVOR.

Native Americans regarded the Sun and Moon as indicators respectively of the active and receptive energies inherent in Nature (see p.24), as well as the measurers of time. They associated solar influences with conscious activity and the exercise of reason and the will, and lunar influences with subconscious activity and the emotional and intuitive aspects of human nature.

The Waxing Moon
*This phase lasts for approximately eleven
days. It is a time of growth and therefore
ideal for developing new ideas and
concentrating your efforts into new projects.*

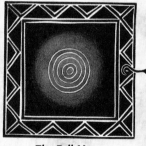

The Full Moon
*Lasting about three days, this is when lunar
power is at its height. It is therefore a good
time for completing what was developed
during the Waxing Moon.*

THE FOUR PHASES

There are four phases in the twenty-nine-day lunar cycle, each one an expression of energy reflecting a particular mode of activity. They can be likened to the phases of growth of a flowering plant through the seasons: the emergence of buds (Waxing Moon), the bursting of flowers (Full Moon), the falling away of flowers (Waning Moon), and the germination of seeds (Dark Moon). The influence of each phase can be felt in two ways: in the formation of personality and in day-to-day life.

The energy expressed by the phase of the Moon at the time of your birth has a strong influence on personality. For instance, someone born during the Dark Moon is likely to be inward-looking, while a person born during the Full Moon may be more expressive. Someone born during a Waxing Moon is likely to have an outgoing nature, while a person born during a Waning Moon may be reserved. Consult a set of Moon tables to discover the phase the Moon was in on your birthday.

In your day-to-day life, the benefits of coming into harmony with the Moon's energies are considerable. Experience the energy of the four phases by consciously working with them. A Native American approach is described below.

The Waning Moon

A time for making changes, this phase lasts for an average of eleven days. Use it to improve and modify, and to dispose of what is no longer needed or wanted.

The Dark Moon

The Moon disappears from the sky for around four days. This is a time for contemplation of what has been achieved, and for germinating the seeds for the new.

THE INFLUENCE OF
ENERGY FLOW

THE MEDICINE WHEEL REFLECTS THE PERFECT
BALANCE OF THE COMPLEMENTARY ACTIVE AND
RECEPTIVE ENERGIES THAT COEXIST IN NATURE.

E nergy flows through Nature in two comple-mentary ways, which can be expressed in terms of active and receptive, or male and female. The active energy principle is linked with the Elements of Fire and Air, and the receptive princi-ple with Water and Earth.

Each of the twelve birth times has an active or receptive energy related to its Elemental Aspect. Traveling around the Wheel, the two energies alternate with each birth time, resulting in an equal balance of active and receptive energies, as in Nature.

Active energy is associated with the Sun and conscious activity. Those whose birth times take this principle prefer to pursue experience. They are conceptual,

outgoing, practical, energetic, and analytical. Receptive energy is associated with the Moon and subconscious activity. Those whose birth times take this principle prefer to attract experience. They are intuitive, reflective, emotional, conserving, and nurturing.

THE WAKAN-TANKA
At the heart of the Wheel lies an S-shape within a circle, the symbol of the life-giving source of everything that comes into physical existence – seemingly out of nothing. Named by the Plains Indians as Wakan-Tanka (Great Power), it can also be perceived as energy coming into form and form reverting to energy in the unending continuity of life.

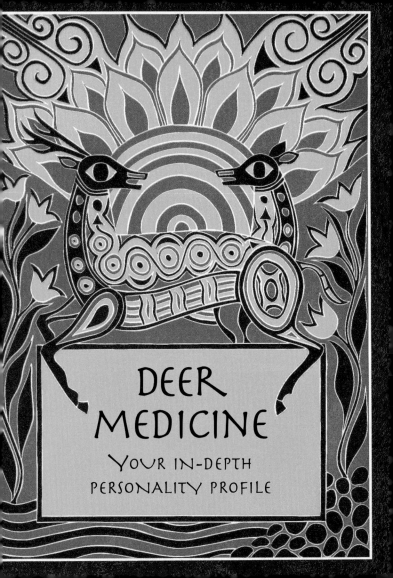

DEER
MEDICINE

YOUR IN-DEPTH
PERSONALITY PROFILE

SEASON OF BIRTH
FLOWERING TIME

THE ENERGIZING POWER OF SPRING REACHES ITS PEAK DURING THE THIRD BIRTH TIME OF THE SEASON, LENDING THOSE BORN THEN THE POWER OF RAPID CHANGE.

Flowering time is one of the twelve birth times, the fundamental division of the year into twelve seasonal periods (see pp.12–13). As the last segment of the Spring cycle, it is a time in which the creative and generative power of Nature is at its height. The trees are in full leaf and many flowers are blooming in the bright, still-lengthening days of this splendid, sensuous time of year.

INFLUENCE OF NATURE

The qualities and characteristics imbued in Nature at this time form the basis of your own nature. So, just as Nature is transforming the Earth, if you were born during Flowering time you too have an inner urge and ability to change whatever comes within your reach. This power might be directed at situations, yourself, or other people.

Your temperament will match the warmth and unpredictability of the season. Just as the influence of the Sun on the Earth is moving toward its peak, you will possess an intensity that enables you to express your creativity rapidly and energetically. However, like a sultry day at this time of year, you are prone to moodiness if beset by setbacks and disappointments that frustrate your efforts to grow. Then, your normally affectionate nature can assume a coolness and standoffishness that can be extremely hurtful to those people who are closest to you.

STAGE OF LIFE

This time of year might be compared to the inquisitive and adventurous nature of youth on the eve of adulthood, when action is taken with determination and courage but often without the understanding that comes with experience and age.

In human development terms, it is a period of life when knowledge is keenly sought after; a time of increasing awareness of the scope and complexity of the world and humanity. Consequently, your warm, affectionate, and eager nature seeks variety and enormous sensory input.

ACHIEVE YOUR POTENTIAL

You are always searching for opportunities to stretch your senses and expand your awareness, so you can comprehend more fully how you fit into the greater scheme of things

Nature's energy
The creative and transforming power of Nature reaches its zenith in this, the last cycle of Spring before the Summer solstice. Many varieties of flowers are blooming and deciduous trees are in full leaf.

and how you can achieve your full potential. Try to use your intuition to open up your understanding beyond the immediate and obvious.

Although you demonstrate abundant vitality when your interest is aroused or when a project is new, you can become lethargic when pressed to complete mundane and routine matters. Set your agile mind and enthusiastic nature to finding ways to motivate yourself to complete tasks you find boring.

"Life is a circle from childhood to childhood; so it is with everything where power moves." Black Elk teaching

BIRTH TOTEM
THE DEER

THE ESSENTIAL NATURE AND CHARACTERISTIC
BEHAVIOR OF THE DEER EXPRESSES THE PERSONALITY
TYPE OF THOSE BORN DURING FLOWERING TIME.

Like the deer, people born during Flowering time are congenial, adaptable, sensitive, and expressive. If you were born at this time, you love variety and thrive on challenges, often giving far more than is expected of you. You appreciate beautiful objects and have expensive tastes. Although both mentally and physically dextrous,

you get bored easily and are readily diverted from routine tasks. A good communicator, you are charming and sociable, and enjoy working as part of a team. You make lively and engaging company, although you can unnerve others by your tendency to change direction suddenly.

You lack patience, persistence, and commitment, which leads you to leap from one relationship or job to another before you have gained all you can from them and without reflecting sufficiently on the consequences of your move. Also, your highly sensitive nature makes you prone to moodiness and irritability.

You are constantly active and like to live on your nerves, but this can lead to physical and mental exhaustion. Even when you are not physically occupied, your mind is busy, making it difficult for you to relax fully. It is essential that you find ways to unwind and ensure that you get enough sleep.

HEALTH MATTERS
Try not to ignore symptoms of poor health, especially if they relate to your most vulnerable areas, which are the lungs and bronchial passages. If you do develop a cough, take care to prevent it from developing into bronchitis.

Deer power
Sensitive, lively, and charming, the deer also expresses the nervous and changeable aspects of the versatile and quick-witted people born at this time.

THE DEER AND
RELATIONSHIPS

SOCIABLE AND ENGAGING, DEER PEOPLE ARE USUALLY
POPULAR. THEY MAKE LIVELY AND CONSIDERATE
PARTNERS BUT MAY PROVE FICKLE IN LOVE.

Naturally friendly creatures, Deer people, like their totem animal, enjoy the company of members of their own sex. If your birth totem is Deer, you make a considerate and compassionate friend, who is seldom demanding and usually sensitive to the difficulties of others. However, you like to talk, tending to know a little about a lot, and to have an answer for almost everything. In consequence, most of your friends tend to be good listeners.

LOVING RELATIONSHIPS

Although Deer people need love and affection, they do not like to be smothered. Blatantly flirtatious, male Deer exudes charm, while female Deer can be tempestuous and alluring. Both male and female Deer

enjoy sex like some people enjoy a good meal, and both are happy to take the sexual initiative.

When Deer people have problems in relationships, it is generally due to their restless and moody nature or their mercenary attitude. For, while they are willing to share most things, money is not one of them. They also tend to be self-indulgent.

COPING WITH DEER

Deer people are impatient, emotional, and vulnerable, so don't be too intense when putting across your point of view to them. They dislike dogmatism and being told what to do and what to think. So the best way to handle Deer – as a friend, lover, employer, or employee – is to cultivate a friendly, informal, and relaxed attitude.

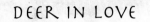

DEER IN LOVE

Deer with Falcon Deer's lively and inventive nature complements Falcon's passion and determination, so both should thrive.

Deer with Beaver Deer's easygoing and restless nature may disturb Beaver's desire for security.

Deer with Deer A lively and adventurous pairing, which will run smoothly if both can learn to work together at the same speed.

Deer with Woodpecker This makes a lively pairing. Woodpecker can overcome Deer's self-centeredness; Deer can inject a sense of fun and purpose.

Deer with Salmon Both are practical opportunists, so they can be unscrupulous together. Their similarities may result in mutual irritability at times.

Deer with Brown Bear Deer's high-spirited vigor can work well with Brown Bear's eye for detail and determination.

Deer with Crow Both are loyal and realistic enough to accept each other's shortcomings.

Deer with Snake Although Snake can be good-natured and considerate, Deer may have difficulty coping with Snake's intensity.

Deer with Owl Deer may find Owl's protectiveness difficult to handle, while Owl may find Deer a little selfish and inconsiderate.

Deer with Goose Deer's freedom-loving nature may resent Goose's zest for disciplined dedication.

Deer with Otter These two vibrant and affable personalities can bond well by doing everything together.

Deer with Wolf Wolf can be an inspiration to Deer if they are dedicated to each other and devoted to achieving similar goals.

DIRECTIONAL TOTEM
THE EAGLE

THE EAGLE SYMBOLIZES THE INFLUENCE OF THE EAST
ON DEER PEOPLE, WHO LOOK TOWARD THE FUTURE AND
LIVE LIFE ACCORDING TO THEIR PRINCIPLES.

A wakening time, Growing time, and Flowering time all fall within the quarter of the Medicine Wheel that is associated with the East Direction or Wind.

The East is aligned with Spring and the dawn of the new day, and it is therefore associated with new beginnings, openness, illumination, and revival. The power of the East's influence is primarily with the spirit, and its principal function is the power of determining. Its totem is the soaring, foresightful eagle.

The specific influence of the East on Deer people is on perception, enabling correct choices to be made. The East Wind in this period may be

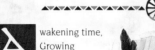

Eagle mask
This Tlingit shaman's headdress represents the eagle, which is associated with being foresightful.

likened to the early experiences of life, and to the qualities of fearlessness and action. It is also associated with the ability to transcend any problems.

EAGLE CHARACTERISTICS
The eagle can fly high in the sky, so Native Americans associated it with lofty ideals and high principles – and with illumination gained from coming closer to the spirit and the source of life. It is also a bird that can

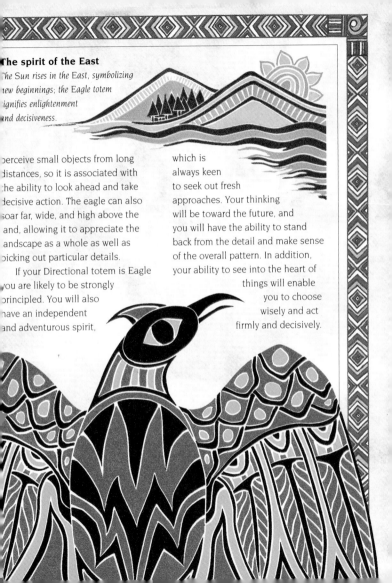

The spirit of the East

The Sun rises in the East, symbolizing new beginnings; the Eagle totem signifies enlightenment and decisiveness.

perceive small objects from long distances, so it is associated with the ability to look ahead and take decisive action. The eagle can also soar far, wide, and high above the land, allowing it to appreciate the landscape as a whole as well as picking out particular details.

If your Directional totem is Eagle you are likely to be strongly principled. You will also have an independent and adventurous spirit, which is always keen to seek out fresh approaches. Your thinking will be toward the future, and you will have the ability to stand back from the detail and make sense of the overall pattern. In addition, your ability to see into the heart of things will enable you to choose wisely and act firmly and decisively.

ELEMENTAL TOTEM
THE BUTTERFLY

LIKE THE BUTTERFLY, WHICH FLITS FROM PLACE TO
PLACE, DEER PEOPLE'S RESTLESS TEMPERAMENT
REQUIRES VARIETY AND ROOM TO MANEUVER.

The Elemental Aspect of Deer people is Air. They share this Aspect with Crow and Otter people, who all therefore belong to the same Elemental family or "clan" (see pp.20–21 for an introduction to the influence of the Elements).

THE BUTTERFLY CLAN

Each Elemental clan has a totem to provide insight into its essential characteristics. The totem of the Elemental clan of Air is Butterfly, which symbolizes a quick, lively, restless, and changeable nature.

The butterfly flits here and there, seeking variety, and settling only where the atmosphere is harmonious.

Free to change
*The butterfly symbolizes the
fundamental quality of the
Element of Air: free movement.*

So, if you belong to this clan, you will have a lively personality and be constantly on the move – physically, mentally, and emotionally.

Quick-witted, thoughtful, and imaginative, you are full of ideas, which you are keen to communicate to others. You dislike being restricted either physically or mentally. You are quick and impatient, and crave stimulation and plenty of opportunity to express yourself.

ELEMENTAL PROFILE

For Deer people, the predominant Elemental Aspect of changeable Air is fundamentally affected by the qualities of your Principal Element – enthusiastic Fire. Consequently, if you were born at this time, you are likely to have an abundance of energy together with a bright, sparkling personality, which is bent on effecting changes in your circumstances and surroundings.

Air of Fire

The Element of Air feeds Fire, generating enthusiasm and expansiveness.

You may have a tendency to bound ahead of yourself, driven by the enthusiasm of Fire and the urge to change that is inherent in Air. So it is that you some-times find yourself in situations for which you are ill-prepared. When faced with setbacks arising from these situations, you can become moody and lethargic.

At times like these, or when you are feeling low or lacking in energy, try the following revitalizing exercise. Find a quiet spot outside, away from the polluting effects of traffic and the activities of others, and for several minutes, breathe slowly and deeply.

With each in-breath, acknowledge that you are drawing into yourself the energizing power of the life-force, which is being absorbed by every cell of your being, revitalizing and refreshing your whole body.

STONE AFFINITY
AGATE

By using the gemstone with which your own essence resonates, you can tap into the power of the Earth itself and awaken the ability you need.

Gemstones are minerals that are formed within the Earth itself in an exceedingly slow but continuous process. Native Americans valued gemstones not only for their beauty but also for being literally part of the Earth, and therefore possessing part of its life force. They regarded gemstones as being "alive" – channelers of energy that could be used in many ways: to heal, to protect, or for meditation.

Every gemstone has a different energy or vibration. On the Medicine Wheel, a stone is associated with each birth time, the energy of which

Polished agate

This highly polished oval agate clearly displays the layered and wavy banding peculiar to this gemstone, which occurs in a wide variety of colors.

resonates with the essence of those born during that time. Because of this energy affiliation, your gemstone can be used to help bring you into harmony with the Earth and to create balance within yourself. It can enhance and develop your good qualities and endow you with the qualities or abilities you need.

ENERGY RESONANCE

Deer people have an affinity with agate – a form of chalcedony with a distinctive banded appearance, which varies tremendously in color and pattern. Agate has a dual nature: it can deflect disturbing vibrations

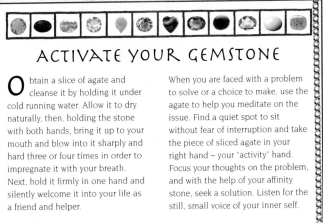

ACTIVATE YOUR GEMSTONE

Obtain a slice of agate and cleanse it by holding it under cold running water. Allow it to dry naturally, then, holding the stone with both hands, bring it up to your mouth and blow into it sharply and hard three or four times in order to impregnate it with your breath. Next, hold it firmly in one hand and silently welcome it into your life as a friend and helper.

When you are faced with a problem to solve or a choice to make, use the agate to help you meditate on the issue. Find a quiet spot to sit without fear of interruption and take the piece of sliced agate in your right hand – your "activity" hand. Focus your thoughts on the problem, and with the help of your affinity stone, seek a solution. Listen for the still, small voice of your inner self.

and resentments caused by humans or the environment, and it can attract positive energies. Regarded as a healing stone by Native Americans, agate is particularly linked to material need and practical matters. This gemstone is also thought to attract loyalty.

If your birth totem is Deer, agate is especially useful in stabilizing your ever-fluctuating emotions. It also enhances your intuitive abilities, making it a valuable aid when trying

to ascertain the best time to begin a new enterprise at work or at home, or the most effective time to make a fundamental change to your life situation.

Agate power

To benefit most from its effect, wear agate next to your skin in the form of a ring, pendant, or necklace.

"The outline of the stone is round; the power of the stone is endless." Lakota Sioux teaching

TREE AFFINITY
ALDER

GAIN A DEEPER UNDERSTANDING OF YOUR OWN NATURE
AND AWAKEN POWERS LYING DORMANT WITHIN YOU BY
RESPECTING AND CONNECTING WITH YOUR AFFINITY TREE.

Trees have an important part to play in the protection of Nature's mechanisms and in the maintenance of the Earth's atmospheric balance, which is essential for the survival of the human race.

Native Americans referred to trees as "standing people" because they stand firm, obtaining strength from their connection with the Earth. They therefore teach us the importance of being grounded, while at the same time listening to, and reaching for, our higher aspirations.

When respected as living beings, trees can provide insight into the workings of Nature and our own inner selves.

On the Medicine Wheel, each birth time is associated with a particular kind of tree, the basic qualities of which complement the nature of those born during that time. Deer people have an affinity with the alder. Essentially a waterside tree, it is therefore associated with the "watery" qualities of emotional energies, which can be fast-flowing and at times turbulent. A key

CONNECT WITH YOUR TREE

Appreciate the beauty of your affinity tree and study its nature carefully, for it has an affinity with your own nature.

The common alder is a hardy, fast-growing tree, with smooth, lustrous, dark-green leaves that last well into the Autumn. At home beside rivers, it thrives in both poor soils and wet conditions, even growing in standing water.

Try the following exercise when you need to revitalize your inner strength. Stand beside your affinity tree. Place the palms of your hands on its trunk and rest your forehead on the backs of your hands. Inhale slowly and let energy from the tree's roots flow through your body. If easily available, obtain a cutting or twig from your affinity tree to keep as a totem or helper.

inherent strength of the alder is its water-resistance, which is due to the oiliness of the wood. Consequently, in times of emotional stress, Deer people can tap into their own powers of resistance by connecting with their tree (see panel above).

EMOTIONAL YET RESILIENT

If your birth totem is Deer, you have a sensitive nature and a tendency towards moodiness during times of stress. This can often provoke you into unconsidered and emotional responses to situations or people. Your feelings at such a time can be so strong as seemingly to carry you along in their current.

However, just as the water-resistant wood of the alder can withstand the pressure of troubled waters, so you can find the power to manage emotional pressures with fortitude. Call on the alder's help and draw on its energy; its resilient quality will renew your inner strength.

"All healing plants are given by Wakan-Tanka; therefore they are holy." Lakota Sioux teaching

COLOR AFFINITY
ORANGE

ENHANCE YOUR POSITIVE QUALITIES BY USING THE
POWER OF YOUR AFFINITY COLOR TO IMPROVE YOUR
EMOTIONAL AND MENTAL STATES.

Each birth time has an affinity with a particular color. This is the color that resonates best with the energies of the people born during that time. Exposure to your affinity color will encourage a positive emotional and mental outlook,

while colors that clash with your affinity color will have a negative effect on your sense of well-being.

Orange resonates with Deer people. Made up of equal parts yellow and red, it combines the influence of both these colors.

Yellow is associated with the mind, and red with vitality and passion, so orange is the embodiment of youthful liveliness,

Color scheme

Let an orange color theme be th thread that runs through your home, from the table settings to the walls and floors.

40

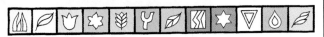

BREATHE IN YOUR COLOR

Take a piece of pale orange or peach-colored paper, cardstock, or fabric. Place it near an open window where it can be seen, and stand directly before it with your legs slightly apart, so that your weight is evenly distributed.

Focus on the color and inhale slowly through the nose. Imagine that the air you breathe in is the color of the card. Hold the breath for a few seconds and feel that color filtering through your entire body, energizing every cell. Breathe out slowly and deliberately. Pause, then begin the sequence again. Continue this rhythmic color breathing for three or four minutes to feel the positive effects.

suggestive of energy, enthusiasm, and ambition. It is a cheerful and optimistic color that invigorates and stimulates creativity. It arouses courage and daring in the drive for exploration and accomplishment.

COLOR BENEFITS

Strengthen your aura and enhance your positive qualities by including shades of orange – peach, apricot, russet – in the interior decor of your home. Spots of color can make all the difference. A peach-tinted lampshade, for example, can alter the ambience of a room, or try filling a bronze vase with deep orange Chinese lanterns.

If you need a confidence boost, wear something that contains orange. Whenever your energies are low, practice the color breathing exercise outlined above to balance your emotions, awaken your creativity, and help you to feel joyful.

"The power of the spirit should be honored with its color." Lakota Sioux teaching

WORKING THE WHEEL
LIFE PATH

Consider your birth profile as a starting point in the development of your character and the achievement of personal fulfillment.

Each of the twelve birth times is associated with a particular path of learning, or with a collection of lessons to be learned through life. By following your path of learning, you will develop strengths in place of weaknesses, achieve a greater sense of harmony with the world, and discover inner peace.

Your path of learning

For Deer people, the first lesson on your path of learning is to overcome impulsiveness. Because of your impatience and your desire to be always on the move, you have a tendency to prefer to do anything rather than nothing. This can sometimes result in your making snap decisions that can be disconcerting to friends and colleagues alike. Next time you have to decide on a course of action try not to be so hasty.
Consider all the

"Each man's road is shown to him within his own heart. There he sees all the truths of life." Cheyenne teaching

options carefully. Compare the situation with a similar one in the past, and if possible, consult all the relevant people. Then evaluate the information and make your decision.

Deer people also need to learn how to discern what is of true value from that which has only limited or short-term benefits. Try not to be deceived by appearances: what seems promising at first glance is often disappointing in the long term.

Your third lesson is to cultivate a more disciplined and consistent approach to life, and to enjoy the accomplishment

of tasks. Your lack of patience with routine and with those less quick-witted than yourself can mean that you do not get the best out of your work or your colleagues, and that you are tempted to change jobs too often to achieve your full career potential. Equally, your fickleness may hamper your ability to find fulfillment in a loving relationship.

WORKING THE WHEEL
MEDICINE POWER

HARNESS THE POWERS OF OTHER BIRTH TIMES TO
TRANSFORM YOUR WEAKNESSES INTO STRENGTHS AND
TO MEET THE CHALLENGES IN YOUR LIFE.

The whole spectrum of human qualities and abilities is represented on the Medicine Wheel. The totems and affinities associated with each birth time represent the basic qualities with which those born at that time are equipped.

Study your path of learning (see pp.42–43) to identify those aspects of your personality that may need to be strengthened, then look at other birth times to discover the totems and affinities that will assist you in this task. For example, your Elemental profile is Air of Fire (see pp.34–35), so for balance you need the stabilizing qualities of Earth and

Complementary affinity
*A key strength of Owl – weak
in Deer – is the ability to see
clearly in times of uncertainty.*

the adaptive nature of Water. Brown Bear's Elemental profile is Earth of Water and Snake's is Water of Earth, so meditate on those birth totems. In addition, you may find it useful to study the profiles of the other two members of your Elemental clan of Butterfly – Crow and Otter – to discover how the same Elemental Aspect can be expressed differently.

Also helpful is the birth totem that sits opposite yours on the Medicine Wheel, which contains qualities that complement or enhance your own. This is known as your complementary affinity, which for Deer people is Owl.

ESSENTIAL STRENGTHS

D escribed below are the essential strengths of each birth totem. To develop a quality that is weak in yourself or that you need to meet a particular challenge, meditate upon the birth totem that contains the attribute you need. Obtain a representation of the relevant totem – a claw, tooth, or feather; a picture, ring, or model. Affirm that the power it represents is within you.

Falcon medicine is the power of keen observation and the ability to act decisively and energetically whenever action is required.

Beaver medicine is the ability to think creatively and laterally – to develop alternative ways of doing or thinking about things.

Deer medicine is characterized by sensitivity to the intentions of others and to that which might be detrimental to your well-being.

Woodpecker medicine is the ability to establish a steady rhythm throughout life and to be tenacious in protecting all that you value.

Salmon medicine is the strength to be determined and courageous in the choice of goals you want to achieve and to have enough stamina to see a task through to the end.

Brown Bear medicine is the ability to be resourceful, hardworking, and dependable in times of need and to draw on inner strength.

Crow medicine is the ability to transform negative or nonproductive situations into positive ones and to transcend limitations.

Snake medicine is the talent to adapt easily to changes in circumstances and to manage transitional phases well.

Owl medicine is the power to see clearly during times of uncertainty and to conduct life consistently, according to long-term plans.

Goose medicine is the courage to do whatever might be necessary to protect your ideals and to adhere to your principles in life.

Otter medicine is the ability to connect with your inner child, to be innovative and idealistic, and to thoroughly enjoy the ordinary tasks and routines of everyday life.

Wolf medicine is the courage to act according to your intuition and instincts rather than your intellect, and to be compassionate.